IT'S NEVER TOO EARLY
TO FIND OUT ABOUT...

SPACE

IT'S NEVER TOO EARLY
TO FIND OUT ABOUT...

SPACE

TIMOTHY KNAPMAN

Illustrated by
KELLY CANBY

Orion
Children's Books

First published in Great Britain in 2015 by Orion Children's Books
An imprint of Hachette Children's Group
A division of Hodder and Stoughton Ltd
Carmelite House
50 Victoria Embankment
London EC4Y 0DZ
An Hachette UK Company

1 3 5 7 9 10 8 6 4 2

Text © Timothy Knapman 2015
Illustrations © Kelly Canby 2015

The right of Timothy Knapman and Kelly Canby to be identified as
author and illustrator of this work has been asserted.

A catalogue record for this book is available from
the British Library.

ISBN 978 1 4440 1575 1

Printed and bound in China

www.orionchildrensbooks.co.uk

To Emma, my chief scientist,
with love
T.K.

CONTENTS

1
Space Ship Earth

You are a space traveller.

This is your space ship.
It's a four and a half billion year old ball
of rock called the Planet Earth.

It may not look like a space ship,
but it flies through space at 107,000
kilometres an hour. So even when
you're completely still, you are travelling
very fast indeed.

But there's no need to hold on tight.
As the Earth zooms along, it also spins
round – at up to 1600 kilometres an hour.
(That's faster than a supersonic aeroplane.)
This spinning is so fast that it creates a force
called **Gravity** which keeps everything
from flying off into space.

Gravity is strong enough to keep the Moon flying round and round the Earth even though the Moon is 384,400 kilometres away. We call this flying round "orbiting".

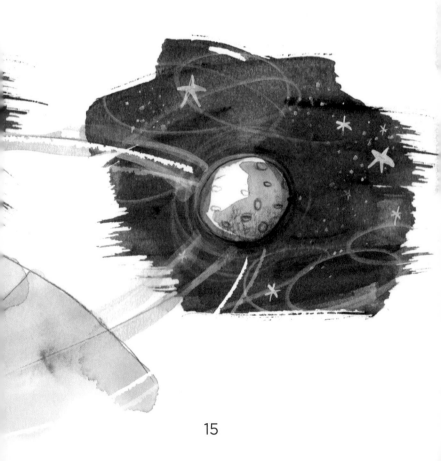

The Earth orbits the Sun, which is
150 million kilometres away. It takes the
Earth a year to go all the way round.

2
Ball of Fire

The Sun is a star – a ball of burning gas.

It is so big that you could fit the Earth
into it a million times over.

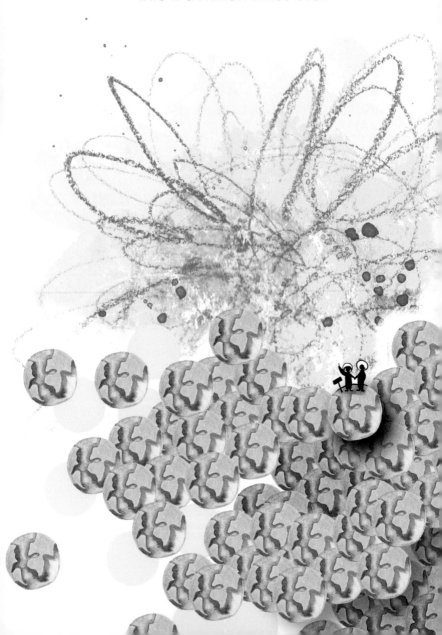

The temperature on its surface is 5,500°C which is 100 times hotter than the hottest place on Earth. At its core it's 15,000,000°C!

So you wouldn't want to go there
on holiday – no matter how much
sun cream you put on!

3
Other Places You Don't Want To Go On Holiday

There are eight planets orbiting the sun.
We call this the Solar System.

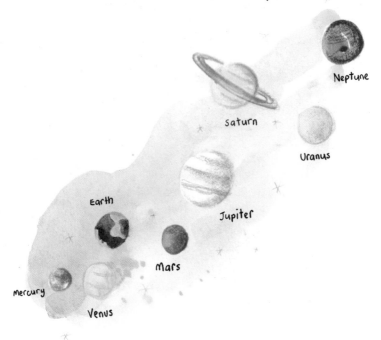

Neptune

Saturn

Uranus

Earth

Jupiter

Mars

Mercury

Venus

The four closest – Mercury, Venus,
the Earth and Mars – are made out of rock.
If you left Earth to explore the others,
you'd find them very unwelcoming.

A day on Mercury is 58 times longer than a day on earth. In daytime, it can get as hot as 427°C. At night it can be as cold as -170°C. The average temperature on Earth is only 16°C.

It's even hotter on Venus, but you wouldn't have a chance to get frazzled up. The air is a thick soup of poison gas so heavy that you'd be squashed flat in no time. There are also clouds of acid flying around.

The air is much thinner on Mars – but it's still
poisonous. Mars is only 20°C at its hottest.
The hottest temperature ever recorded on
our planet was nearly three times hotter.
It hasn't rained there for billions of years so
you wouldn't need to take your umbrella.

Beyond Mars, there's a belt of asteroids – bits of smashed up rock. You'd have to steer carefully through them if you wanted to voyage further out.

Then you'd reach the four gas giants –
Jupiter, Saturn, Uranus and Neptune.
They are huge balls of gas swirling
around centres of solid rock.

Jupiter is the largest of all the planets. It is famous for its great, oval-shaped red spot. The spot is 12,000 by 25,000 km – the size of two Planet Earths! The spot is actually a storm that has been raging for 350 years – long enough to ruin any picnic.

All the gas giants have rings around them –
made up of ice and bits of rock.
The ones on Saturn are the largest.

Uranus is named after the Ancient Greek
god of the heavens, but the man who first
spotted it wanted to call it "George's Planet"
after King George III.

Neptune is the windiest planet. Its winds blow five times faster than the fastest winds on Earth. You'd have to hold on very tightly if you wanted to fly a kite there.

4
How Do We Know All This?

People have always looked up at the stars and wondered about them. For more than three thousand years, we've been writing down lists of the stars we've seen.

For most of that time, astronomers (that's people who study the stars) had to peer up into the night sky with their naked eyes. They must have got very sore. But four hundred years ago, telescopes were invented.

This is a **telescope** – a long tube with glass lenses at both ends. The lenses work like a magnifying glass, making it much easier to study the stars and planets even though they're a long, long way away.

After a while, just looking wasn't enough.
In 1961, the Russian Yuri Gagarin became
the first man in space.

Only eight years later, the USA landed
two men, Neil Armstrong and Buzz Aldrin,
on the Moon.

But space exploration can be dangerous, so nowadays we send out remote-controlled space ships, called **probes**, to investigate the planets and stars for us. This is the Mars Exploration Rover.

camera →

← antenna

solar panels

← Robot arm

Flat solar panels, which look a bit like wings,
trap the energy of the sun and turn it into
electricity to power the Rover. Its camera
and robot arm allow scientists back
on Earth to study the surface of Mars
in great detail.

Telescopes in space can see
much further than the ones down on Earth.
This is the Hubble Space Telescope.

It cost $1.5 billion (the cost of about seven blockbuster movies) but for the last 25 years it has shown us many galaxies and stars we didn't know were there.

It has also helped us work out the age of the universe. (It's 13.7 billion years old – you'd need a seriously big birthday cake to fit that many candles on!)

5
The Great Beyond

The Sun is only one of many, many stars.

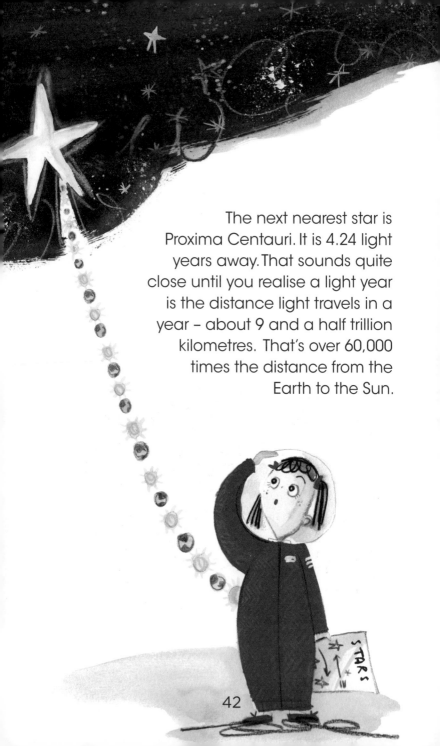

The next nearest star is Proxima Centauri. It is 4.24 light years away. That sounds quite close until you realise a light year is the distance light travels in a year – about 9 and a half trillion kilometres. That's over 60,000 times the distance from the Earth to the Sun.

STARS

42

Proxima Centauri is a brown dwarf – a small star only about an eighth as big as our Sun.

Proxima CENTAURI

BETELGEUSE

But stars come in many sizes. Betelgeuse, for instance, is a red supergiant 640 light years away. It is 500 times bigger than the Sun.

Stars don't last forever. When a big star like Betelgeuse runs out of fuel, it collapses in a gigantic explosion called a Supernova.

All that's left after the explosion is a small point in space whose gravity is so great that it pulls everything into it, including light. This is called a **Black Hole**.

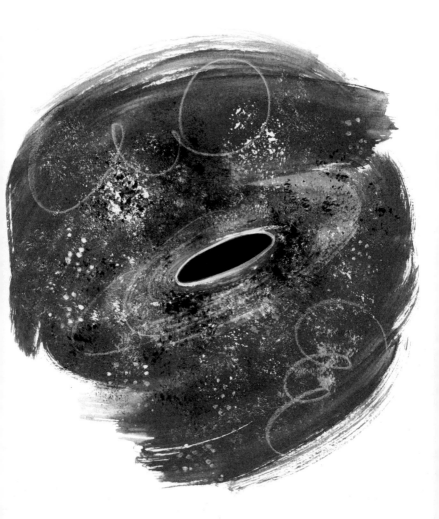

Stars are grouped together in **galaxies**.
This is the Milky Way galaxy, a great spiral
made up of 200 billion stars. It is more
than 100,000 light years across.
If you look really closely,
you might just see
our Sun.

There are at least 170 billion galaxies
in the Universe – and they come in
all sorts of shapes and sizes – spiral like
ours, elliptical, colliding, irregular.

6
Aliens

People have often wondered about
life on other planets.

Many books, films and television series have been made imagining what aliens from outer space would look like, and what would happen if we ever met them.

Some people claim to
have seen **UFO**s – Unidentified Flying
Objects – that they think are alien space
ships. There has, however, never been any
definite proof of human contact with aliens.

The universe is amazingly huge
so it is very unlikely that the Earth is
the only planet with life on it.

We know there are at least
700 other planets out there,
orbiting stars as the Earth does.

However, they are so very, very far away
that there's very little chance we will ever
make contact.

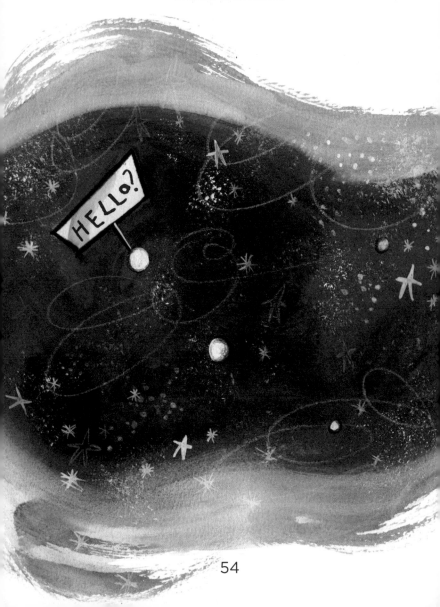

7
The Big Bang

Scientists believe that the Universe began from one teeny, tiny super-hot point.

Suddenly, everything there is –
space, energy and matter – came flying
out of this tiny point. This moment is called
"the Big Bang".

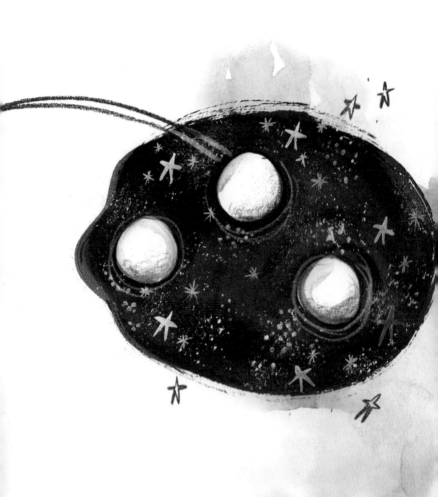

The stars started forming 50 million years or so later. Nine billion years after the Big Bang, the **Solar System** was formed.

The Universe is still expanding.

8
Nothing Lasts Forever

No one knows how the Universe will end,
but there are a number of interesting
theories. Take your pick!

The Big Chill – the Universe will continue to expand until it runs out of energy and goes dark.

The Big Rip – the Universe will expand very fast, tearing galaxies, stars and planets apart.

The Big Crunch – instead of expanding, the Universe will shrink until everything is concentrated in one teeny, tiny superhot point. Sounds familiar?

Some people say that another Big Bang will then happen and a whole new Universe will be formed.